THE

STRATEGIC

INVESTOR....

"Building Wealth Through Stock Market Wisdom"

CHAPTERS :-

Chapter 1: Introduction to Strategic Investing

Investing in the stock market can be a rewarding endeavor, but it's not without its challenges. To navigate the complex and often unpredictable world of stocks successfully, you must adopt a strategic approach. This chapter introduces you to the fundamentals of strategic investing and lays the groundwork for your journey to building wealth through stock market wisdom.

Why Invest?

The Financial Goals Puzzle

The first step in your investment journey is to answer a fundamental question: Why do you want to invest? Your motivation might be to secure a comfortable retirement, purchase a home, send your children to college, or achieve financial independence. Each of these goals requires a unique investment strategy, and understanding your objectives is crucial to crafting the right approach.

The Power of Compound Interest

Investing allows your money to grow over time through the magic of compound interest. Compound interest is the interest earned not only on your initial investment but also on the interest it accumulates over time. The longer you invest, the more powerful this compounding effect becomes. This is why starting early and staying invested for the long term can greatly boost your wealth.

The Importance of Strategy

The Difference Between Investing and Speculating

Investing is not the same as speculating. While speculation involves making bets on short-term price movements, investing focuses on building long-term wealth through a systematic and disciplined approach. Strategic investors base their decisions on research, analysis, and a well-thought-out plan.

Emotions and Investing

One of the biggest challenges investors face is managing their emotions. Fear and greed can drive impulsive decisions that lead to losses. A strategic investor learns to recognize and control these emotions, sticking to their plan regardless of market volatility.

Your Investment Journey

The Investment Pyramid

Think of your investment journey as building a pyramid. At the base are low-risk, stable investments like savings accounts and bonds. As you move up the pyramid, you encounter higher-risk, higher-reward investments like stocks and real estate. Your investment strategy should align with your risk tolerance and financial goals.

Time Horizon Matters

Your time horizon—the length of time you plan to invest—impacts your investment choices. Long-term investors can afford to take on more risk, while short-term investors may prefer safer assets. Understanding your time horizon is essential for crafting a suitable investment strategy.

Conclusion

As you embark on your journey to becoming a strategic investor, remember that success in the stock market is not about luck; it's about strategy and discipline. This chapter has provided you with the foundational knowledge to start your investment journey with confidence. In the chapters that follow, we will delve deeper into the strategies and techniques that will help you achieve your financial goals.

Chapter 2: The Psychology of Investing

Investing in the stock market isn't just about numbers and analysis; it's also about understanding and managing the psychological aspects of decision-making. In this chapter, we will explore the powerful influence of psychology on your investment choices and provide strategies for managing your emotions to become a more successful investor.

Emotions and Investing

The Emotional Rollercoaster

Investing can be an emotional rollercoaster. The stock market is inherently volatile, and price fluctuations can trigger a range of emotions, from excitement and overconfidence during bull markets to fear and panic during bear markets. These emotions can lead to impulsive decisions that may harm your portfolio.

Common Emotional Biases

Investors often fall prey to cognitive biases that cloud their judgment. These biases include:

- **Overconfidence:** Believing that you're a better investor than you actually are.
- **Loss Aversion:** Feeling the pain of losses more intensely than the pleasure of gains.
- **Herding Behavior:** Following the crowd instead of making independent decisions.
- **Confirmation Bias:** Seeking information that confirms pre-existing beliefs.

Recognizing these biases is the first step toward overcoming them.

Managing Your Emotions

Develop a Long-Term Perspective

One of the most effective ways to manage emotions is to adopt a long-term perspective. Understand that short-term market fluctuations are a normal part of investing, and focus on your long-term financial goals. This perspective can help you stay calm during market turbulence.

Create a Solid Investment Plan

Having a well-defined investment plan can provide structure and discipline. Your plan should outline your goals, risk tolerance, and the strategies you'll use. When emotions run high, refer back to your plan to stay on course.

Diversification and Risk Management

Diversifying your portfolio across different asset classes and industries can help reduce risk and volatility. Knowing that your investments are spread out can ease anxiety during market downturns.

Set Realistic Expectations

Avoid chasing unrealistic returns or trying to time the market perfectly. Understand that investing involves periods of both gains and losses. Realistic expectations can help you stay grounded.

Behavioral Techniques

Keep Detailed Records

Maintaining a trading journal can help you track your decisions and emotions. Reviewing past trades and their outcomes can provide valuable insights into your behavior and help you improve.

Practice Mindfulness

Mindfulness techniques, such as meditation and deep breathing, can help you stay calm and focused during turbulent market moments. These practices can enhance your emotional resilience.

Conclusion

Mastering the psychology of investing is a crucial step on your journey to becoming a strategic investor. By recognizing the emotional challenges that can arise, developing strategies to manage your emotions, and practicing mindfulness, you can make more rational and informed investment decisions. In the next chapter, we will explore the importance of setting clear financial goals and how they influence your investment strategy.

Chapter 3: Setting Financial Goals

Before you embark on your journey as an investor, it's essential to define clear financial goals. Your investment strategy should align with these objectives, guiding your decisions and helping you stay on track. In this chapter, we will explore the process of setting meaningful financial goals and how they shape your investment plan.

The Importance of Goals

A Sense of Purpose

Financial goals give your investment journey purpose and direction. They provide you with a clear reason to invest and a roadmap for achieving your desired financial outcomes.

Motivation and Discipline

Having specific goals can motivate you to save and invest consistently. When you know what you're working toward, it becomes easier to stay disciplined and make informed financial decisions.

Types of Financial Goals

Short-Term Goals

Short-term financial goals typically have a time horizon of one to three years. They might include saving for a vacation, purchasing a new car, or building an emergency fund. Short-term goals require a focus on liquidity and safety.

Intermediate-Term Goals

Intermediate-term goals span three to ten years and often involve larger expenses, such as buying a home, funding a child's education, or starting a business. These goals may require a balanced approach to risk and return.

Long-term financial goals extend beyond ten years and are often centered on retirement planning. Building a substantial nest egg for retirement is a common long-term goal. Long-term goals can accommodate more risk, as there is more time to weather market fluctuations.

SMART Goals

To make your financial goals more effective, consider the SMART criteria:

- **Specific:** Clearly define what you want to achieve.
- **Measurable:** Establish metrics to track your progress.
- **Achievable:** Set realistic goals that you can attain.
- **Relevant:** Ensure your goals align with your values and priorities.
- **Time-Bound:** Set a specific timeline for achieving your goals.

Creating Your Financial Goals

Step 1: Identify Your Goals

Start by identifying your financial objectives. Consider both short-term and long-term goals, and be as specific as possible. For example, rather than saying, "I want to retire comfortably," specify a retirement age and the income you aim to generate.

Step 2: Prioritize Your Goals

Determine which goals are most important to you. Not all goals are equal in urgency or significance. Prioritizing helps you allocate your resources effectively.

Step 3: Quantify Your Goals

Attach a dollar amount to each goal. Calculate how much money you need to achieve your objectives. This step will inform your savings and investment targets.

Step 4: Set Deadlines

Assign realistic deadlines to each goal. Knowing when you want to achieve them will influence your investment horizon and strategy.

Conclusion

Setting financial goals is the foundation of successful investing. Your goals serve as a compass, guiding you toward the financial future you desire. With SMART goals in place, you'll have a clear roadmap to follow as you move forward in your investment journey. In the following chapters, we will explore strategies for managing risk and creating a well-balanced investment portfolio tailored to your specific goals.

Chapter 4: Risk Management Strategies

Investing in the stock market offers the potential for significant returns, but it also comes with inherent risks. To navigate these risks and protect your investment capital, you must implement effective risk management strategies. In this chapter, we will explore various approaches to managing risk in your investment portfolio.

Understanding Risk

Risk vs. Reward

In investing, risk and reward are closely related. Generally, assets with higher potential returns also come with higher levels of risk. Understanding this trade-off is essential for making informed investment decisions.

Types of Risk

There are various types of risk in investing, including:

- **Market Risk:** The risk of losing money due to broad market movements.
- **Company Risk:** The risk associated with individual companies or stocks.
- **Interest Rate Risk:** The risk that changes in interest rates will affect the value of bonds and other fixed-income securities.
- **Inflation Risk:** The risk that rising prices will erode the purchasing power of your investments.
- **Liquidity Risk:** The risk of not being able to sell an investment quickly at a fair price.

Risk Management Strategies

Diversification

Diversification involves spreading your investments across different asset classes, industries, and geographic regions. By doing so, you can reduce the impact of poor performance in any single investment on your overall portfolio. Diversification is often referred to as the "don't put all your eggs in one basket" strategy.

Asset Allocation

Asset allocation is the process of determining how to distribute your investments among different asset classes, such as stocks, bonds, and cash equivalents. Your choice of asset allocation should align with your risk tolerance and financial goals.

Risk Tolerance Assessment

Understanding your risk tolerance is crucial. It refers to your ability and willingness to withstand fluctuations in the value of your investments. Risk tolerance can vary from person to person and should be assessed carefully to ensure your investments match your comfort level.

Stop-Loss Orders

A stop-loss order is a pre-set price at which you instruct your broker to sell a stock. It can help limit potential losses by automatically selling a stock if it falls below a certain price. However, it's essential to set stop-loss levels thoughtfully to avoid being triggered by short-term market fluctuations.

Dollar-Cost Averaging

Dollar-cost averaging involves regularly investing a fixed amount of money into the market at predetermined intervals, regardless of market conditions. This strategy can help reduce the impact of market volatility by allowing you to buy more shares when prices are low and fewer shares when prices are high.

Risk Management Tools

Consider using risk management tools such as options, futures, and insurance products to hedge against specific risks in your portfolio. These tools can be complex and may require specialized knowledge, so seek professional advice if you plan to use them.

Conclusion

Effectively managing risk is a critical component of successful investing. By implementing a combination of diversification, asset allocation, risk tolerance assessment, and risk management tools, you can protect your investment capital while pursuing your financial goals.

Chapter 5: Asset Allocation

Asset allocation is a critical component of successful investing. It involves the strategic distribution of your investment capital among different asset classes, such as stocks, bonds, cash equivalents, and alternative investments. In this chapter, we will explore the importance of asset allocation and how to create a well-balanced investment portfolio.

The Significance of Asset Allocation

Balancing Risk and Reward

Asset allocation is all about balancing the trade-off between risk and reward. Different asset classes offer varying levels of risk and return potential. By diversifying your investments across these classes, you can manage risk while aiming for your financial goals.

Achieving Your Objectives

Asset allocation plays a central role in helping you achieve your financial objectives. It ensures that your investments are aligned with your goals, risk tolerance, and time horizon.

Asset Classes

Stocks

Stocks represent ownership in a company and offer the potential for capital appreciation. They are known for their higher volatility but also tend to provide greater long-term returns.

Bonds

Bonds are debt securities issued by governments, corporations, or other entities. They offer regular interest payments and are generally considered lower risk than stocks. Bonds can provide income and stability to a portfolio.

Cash Equivalents

Cash equivalents include investments like money market funds and Treasury bills. They are highly liquid and low risk, making them suitable for short-term needs and emergencies.

Alternative Investments

Alternative investments encompass a wide range of assets, including real estate, commodities, hedge funds, and private equity. They can provide diversification and unique return opportunities but often come with higher complexity and risk.

The Asset Allocation Process

Assessing Risk Tolerance

Before determining your asset allocation, assess your risk tolerance. Your comfort level with risk should guide your choices. Conservative investors may favor a higher allocation to bonds and cash equivalents, while aggressive investors may allocate more to stocks.

Setting Goals

Your financial goals also play a role in asset allocation. Goals with longer time horizons may allow for a more significant equity allocation, while short-term goals may require a more conservative approach.

Building a Diversified Portfolio

Diversification is a key principle of asset allocation. By spreading your investments across various asset classes, you can reduce the impact of poor performance in any one area. An ideal portfolio is one that combines assets with low correlations.

Regular Rebalancing

Over time, market fluctuations can cause your portfolio to deviate from your intended asset allocation. Regularly rebalancing involves selling assets that have exceeded their target allocation and buying those that have fallen below, restoring your desired balance.

Modern Portfolio Theory

Modern Portfolio Theory (MPT) is an investment framework that emphasizes the importance of asset allocation. MPT suggests that investors can achieve an optimal level of risk and return by constructing a diversified portfolio that considers the correlation between asset classes.

Conclusion

Asset allocation is a fundamental element of strategic investing. By carefully selecting the right mix of asset classes based on your risk tolerance, financial goals, and time horizon, you can build a portfolio that offers a balanced approach to managing risk and pursuing returns. In the following chapters, we will explore specific strategies for selecting individual investments within each asset class and constructing a well-rounded investment portfolio.

Chapter 6: Stock Market Fundamentals

Before diving into the world of stock market investing, it's crucial to build a solid foundation by understanding the fundamentals. This chapter will introduce you to the essential concepts, terminologies, and principles that underpin the stock market.

What Is a Stock?

Ownership in a Company

At its core, a stock represents ownership in a company. When you purchase a share of stock, you become a shareholder, which means you have a claim on a portion of the company's assets and earnings.

Types of Stocks

There are two main types of stocks:

- **Common Stocks:** These grant shareholders voting rights and a share of the company's profits (dividends). Common stockholders have a say in the company's decisions at shareholder meetings.
- **Preferred Stocks:** Preferred stockholders have a higher claim on the company's assets and earnings but typically do not have voting rights. They often receive fixed dividend payments.

How Stocks are Traded

Stock Exchanges

Stocks are traded on stock exchanges, which are organized and regulated marketplaces where buyers and sellers come together to conduct transactions. Major stock exchanges include the New York Stock Exchange (NYSE)

Ticker Symbols

Each publicly traded company is identified by a unique ticker symbol, a combination of letters often abbreviated from the company's name. Ticker symbols are used to locate and trade specific stocks.

Stock Market Participants

Investors

Investors are individuals or institutions that buy and hold stocks for the long term, with the goal of building wealth and earning returns through capital appreciation and dividends.

Traders

Traders, on the other hand, aim to profit from short-term price fluctuations. They may buy and sell stocks within minutes, hours, or days, using various trading strategies.

Stock Indices

Dow Jones Industrial Average (DJIA)

The DJIA is one of the oldest and most widely followed stock market indices. It tracks the performance of 30 large, publicly traded companies, providing a snapshot of the U.S. stock market.

S&P 500

The S&P 500 is a broader index that includes 500 of the largest U.S. companies. It is considered a more comprehensive representation of the U.S. stock market's performance.

NASDAQ Composite

The NASDAQ Composite Index includes more than 3,000 companies, primarily in the technology sector. It is known for its heavy representation of tech giants like Apple, Amazon, and Microsoft.

Stock Market Orders

Market Orders

A market order is an instruction to buy or sell a stock at the current market price. It guarantees the execution of the order but does not specify the price.

Limit Orders

A limit order allows investors to set a specific price at which they are willing to buy or sell a stock. The order will only execute if the market reaches the specified price.

Conclusion

Understanding stock market fundamentals is the first step toward becoming a successful investor. With this knowledge, you'll be better equipped to navigate the world of stocks, make informed decisions, and communicate effectively within the financial markets. In the following chapters, we will delve deeper into various stock selection strategies and investment approaches that will help you achieve your financial goals.

Chapter 7: Stock Selection Strategies

One of the key challenges in stock market investing is choosing the right stocks to include in your portfolio. This chapter explores various stock selection strategies, each with its own approach and criteria for identifying promising investments.

Fundamental Analysis

Understanding the Basics

Fundamental analysis involves evaluating a company's financial health and prospects to determine its intrinsic value. Key elements of fundamental analysis include:

- **Financial Statements:** Analyzing income statements, balance sheets, and cash flow statements.
- **Earnings per Share (EPS):** Assessing a company's profitability.
- **Price-to-Earnings (P/E) Ratio:** Comparing a company's stock price to its earnings per share.
- **Dividend Yield:** Evaluating the dividend income potential.

The Value Investing Approach

Value investors seek to buy stocks that are undervalued compared to their intrinsic value. This approach, famously practiced by Warren Buffett, involves looking for stocks trading at a discount and holding them for the long term.

Technical Analysis

Chart Patterns and Trends

Technical analysis relies on historical price and volume data to predict future stock movements. Key components of technical analysis include:

- **Chart Patterns:** Identifying patterns like head and shoulders, double tops, and triangles.
- **Trends:** Analyzing price trends, such as uptrends and downtrends.
- **Indicators:** Using tools like moving averages, relative strength, and MACD to make trading decisions.

The Momentum Trading Approach

Momentum traders focus on stocks that are currently trending, aiming to profit from short-term price movements. They buy stocks that have been performing well and sell those that have been underperforming.

Growth Investing

Identifying Growth Stocks

Growth investors seek companies with strong potential for future earnings growth. Key factors include:

- **Revenue Growth:** Identifying companies with increasing sales.
- **Earnings Growth:** Looking for companies with growing profits.
- **Market Opportunity:** Assessing the size of the market the company operates in.

The Growth at a Reasonable Price (GARP) Approach

GARP investors combine elements of both value and growth investing. They look for companies that are growing but still trading at reasonable valuations.

Income Investing

Dividend Stocks

Income investors focus on stocks that pay regular dividends. These dividends provide a consistent income stream, making them attractive for those seeking income in addition to capital appreciation.

The Dividend Aristocrats

Some income investors specifically target stocks known as "Dividend Aristocrats," which are companies with a history of consistently increasing their dividends year after year.

Quality Investing

Assessing Quality Metrics

Quality investors prioritize stocks from financially stable companies with strong management teams and competitive advantages. They look at metrics like:

- **Return on Equity (ROE):** Evaluating a company's profitability.
- **Debt-to-Equity Ratio:** Assessing a company's financial leverage.
- **Competitive Positioning:** Analyzing a company's position within its industry.

Conclusion

Choosing the right stock selection strategy depends on your financial goals, risk tolerance, and investment horizon. Each approach has its strengths and weaknesses, and successful investors often combine elements from multiple strategies to build a diversified and well-rounded portfolio. In the following chapters, we will explore advanced investment strategies and tactics to help you fine-tune your stock selection process.

Chapter 8: Long-Term vs. Short-Term Investing

Investors often face the decision of whether to adopt a long-term or short-term investment approach. In this chapter, we will explore the differences between these two strategies, their advantages, and considerations to help you determine which approach aligns best with your financial goals.

Defining Long-Term and Short-Term Investing

Long-Term Investing

Long-term investing typically involves holding assets for an extended period, often several years or decades. The primary focus is on building wealth gradually over time through capital appreciation and compounding.

Short-Term Investing

Short-term investing, on the other hand, involves buying and selling assets with the goal of profiting from short-term price fluctuations. This approach may span days, weeks, or a few months and is characterized by more active trading.

Advantages of Long-Term Investing

Compound Interest

Long-term investors benefit from the power of compounding. As your investments generate returns, those returns are reinvested, leading to exponential growth over time. This compounding effect can significantly increase your wealth.

Lower Transaction Costs

Long-term investing typically incurs lower transaction costs compared to frequent trading. Frequent trading can erode profits through fees and taxes.

Reduced Emotional Stress

Long-term investors may experience less emotional stress compared to short-term traders who face the pressure of monitoring the market daily. A long-term perspective allows for a more relaxed approach.

Advantages of Short-Term Investing

Liquidity

Short-term investing provides more liquidity, allowing investors to access their funds quickly if needed. This flexibility can be advantageous in responding to changing financial circumstances.

Capitalizing on Market Volatility

Short-term traders aim to profit from market volatility by buying low and selling high. They can take advantage of short-term price movements that may not affect long-term investors.

Adaptability

Short-term traders have the flexibility to adjust their strategies quickly in response to changing market conditions, news events, or economic indicators.

Considerations When Choosing

Financial Goals

Consider your financial goals when choosing between long-term and short-term investing. Long-term goals, such as retirement planning or building wealth over decades, are better suited to a long-term approach. Short-term goals, like funding a vacation or covering immediate expenses, may warrant a short-term strategy.

Risk Tolerance

Your risk tolerance plays a significant role. Long-term investors can afford to take on more risk because they have time to recover from market downturns. Short-term investors may need to be more risk-averse.

Time Commitment

Consider the time commitment required for each approach. Long-term investing demands less active management and research, while short-term trading often requires constant monitoring of the market.

Combining Both Approaches

It's worth noting that many investors combine long-term and short-term strategies within their portfolios. This approach, known as "core and satellite" investing, involves maintaining a long-term core portfolio while adding short-term positions for specific opportunities or goals.

Conclusion

The choice between long-term and short-term investing should align with your financial objectives, risk tolerance, and time commitment. There is no one-size-fits-all approach, and both strategies can be viable depending on your circumstances. Understanding the advantages and considerations of each approach will help you make informed decisions that support your financial goals. In the following chapters, we will explore specific techniques and tactics for implementing each approach effectively.

Chapter 9: Value Investing

Value investing is a timeless investment strategy that has been practiced successfully by some of the most renowned investors, including Benjamin Graham and Warren Buffett. In this chapter, we will delve into the principles and techniques of value investing, providing you with the tools to identify undervalued stocks and build a value-oriented portfolio.

Understanding Value Investing

The Core Principle

At its core, value investing seeks to buy stocks that are trading at a price significantly below their intrinsic or true value. Value investors believe that markets often overreact to news and events, causing stocks to become mispriced.

Margin of Safety

Central to value investing is the concept of a "margin of safety." This means purchasing stocks at a price well below their intrinsic value to protect against unforeseen market downturns or company-specific issues.

Key Elements of Value Investing

Fundamental Analysis

Value investors rely heavily on fundamental analysis to assess a company's financial health. This includes examining:

- **Earnings:** Assessing a company's profitability and growth prospects.
- **Financial Statements:** Analyzing income statements, balance sheets, and cash flow statements.
- **Price-to-Earnings (P/E) Ratio:** Comparing a company's stock price to its earnings per share.
- **Book Value:** Assessing the value of a company's assets minus its liabilities.

Qualitative Factors

Beyond financial metrics, value investors consider qualitative factors such as a company's competitive advantage, management quality, and industry position. These factors help determine a company's intrinsic value.

Value Investing Strategies

Contrarian Investing

Contrarian investors often go against prevailing market sentiment. When others are selling in fear, contrarians may see an opportunity to buy undervalued stocks.

Dividend Investing

Many value investors favor stocks that pay dividends. Dividend stocks can provide a consistent income stream and are often associated with more mature, stable companies.

The Value Investing Process

Stock Screening

Value investors use various screening criteria to identify potential investments. Common criteria include low P/E ratios, low price-to-book ratios, and high dividend yields.

In-Depth Analysis

Once potential value stocks are identified, thorough research and analysis are conducted to assess their intrinsic value. This may involve detailed financial modeling and understanding the company's competitive position.

Patience and Discipline

Value investors are known for their patience and discipline. They are willing to wait for the market to recognize the true value of their investments, which may take time.

The Warren Buffett Approach

Warren Buffett, one of the most famous value investors, follows a long-term value investing approach. He emphasizes the importance of buying quality companies with enduring competitive advantages (often referred to as "economic moats") and holding them for the long term.

Conclusion

Value investing offers a methodical and disciplined approach to stock market investing. By focusing on fundamental analysis, qualitative factors, and a margin of safety, value investors aim to build a portfolio of undervalued stocks with the potential for significant long-term gains. While value investing requires patience and research, it has a proven track record of success among investors who are willing to follow its principles. In the following chapters, we will explore other investment strategies and approaches to help you further refine your investing skills.

Chapter 10: Growth Investing

Growth investing is a dynamic approach to stock market investing that focuses on identifying companies with substantial growth potential. In this chapter, we will explore the principles, strategies, and techniques of growth investing, enabling you to spot promising growth stocks and construct a growth-oriented portfolio.

Understanding Growth Investing

The Core Principle

At its core, growth investing seeks to invest in companies that are expected to experience above-average growth in revenue, earnings, or other key metrics. Growth investors believe that such companies have the potential to deliver substantial capital appreciation.

Growth vs. Value

Growth investing stands in contrast to value investing, which seeks out undervalued stocks trading below their intrinsic value. While value investors prioritize safety and stability, growth investors are more inclined to accept higher valuations in exchange for growth potential.

Key Elements of Growth Investing

Identifying Growth Stocks

Growth investors focus on identifying growth stocks with the following characteristics:

- **Revenue Growth:** Companies with a history of strong and consistent revenue growth.
- **Earnings Growth:** Consistently increasing profits and earnings per share.
- **Market Opportunity:** Operating in industries with significant growth potential.
- **Competitive Positioning:** Demonstrating a competitive edge or unique product/service.

High Valuations

Growth stocks are often associated with higher valuations, such as higher price-to-earnings (P/E) ratios. Investors are willing to pay a premium for the expected future growth of these companies.

Growth Investing Strategies

Growth at a Reasonable Price (GARP)

Some growth investors adopt a GARP strategy, combining elements of both value and growth investing. They seek companies with growth potential that are trading at reasonable valuations.

Momentum Investing

Momentum investors focus on stocks that have been performing well in the short term. They aim to capitalize on existing market trends and continue riding the upward momentum.

The Growth Investing Process

Screening for Growth Stocks

Growth investors often use screening criteria to identify potential investments. These criteria may include revenue and earnings growth rates, forward P/E ratios, and industry prospects.

Research and Due Diligence

Thorough research is essential to assess a company's growth prospects accurately. This includes analyzing financial statements, understanding the industry, and evaluating competitive positioning.

Risk Management

Growth investing comes with inherent risks, as the market may not always reward high-growth companies with increasing stock prices. Risk management strategies, including portfolio diversification, are crucial.

Conclusion

Growth investing is a dynamic and forward-looking approach to stock market investing. By focusing on companies with substantial growth potential, growth investors aim to capitalize on future earnings and revenue expansion. While growth investing can be rewarding, it also carries higher risk due to the often premium valuations associated with growth stocks. As with any investment strategy, it's important to align growth investing with your financial goals, risk tolerance, and time horizon. In the following chapters, we will explore additional investment strategies and tactics to help you refine your investment approach.

Chapter 11: Income Investing

Income investing is a strategy focused on generating a steady stream of income from your investments. This chapter explores the principles, strategies, and techniques of income investing, helping you identify income-generating assets and construct an income-focused portfolio.

Understanding Income Investing

The Core Principle

Income investing prioritizes assets that provide regular income payments, such as interest or dividends. The goal is to generate a reliable cash flow from your investments, which can be used to cover living expenses or reinvested for growth.

Income vs. Capital Appreciation

Income investing differs from strategies that primarily seek capital appreciation. While capital appreciation aims for long-term growth in the value of assets, income investing seeks to maximize current income.

Key Elements of Income Investing

Income-Generating Assets

Income investors focus on assets that offer income potential, including:

- **Dividend Stocks:** Stocks of companies that pay regular dividends.
- **Bonds:** Fixed-income securities that pay periodic interest.
- **Real Estate Investment Trusts (REITs):** Real estate investments that generate rental income.
- **Preferred Stocks:** Stocks with a fixed dividend rate.
- **High-Yield Bonds:** Bonds with higher interest rates but potentially higher risk.

Dependable Income

Income investors prioritize dependable income streams, which means they often select assets from stable, dividend-paying companies or bonds with high credit ratings.

Income Investing Strategies

Dividend Growth Investing

Dividend growth investors focus on stocks of companies with a history of consistently increasing their dividend payments. These companies often have strong financials and a commitment to returning value to shareholders.

High-Yield Investing

High-yield investors seek assets with above-average income potential. While this approach can provide attractive income, it may come with higher risk due to the possibility of defaults or dividend cuts.

The Income Investing Process

Asset Selection

Income investors carefully select income-generating assets that align with their income goals, risk tolerance, and time horizon. Asset selection may involve screening for high-dividend stocks or researching bond offerings.

Diversification

Diversification is crucial in income investing to spread risk across different income sources. A diversified income portfolio may include a mix of dividend stocks, bonds, and other income-generating assets.

Income Reinvestment

Income generated from investments can be reinvested to buy additional income-generating assets, which can accelerate the growth of your income stream over time.

Risk Management

Income investors should be aware of the risks associated with income-generating assets, such as the risk of bond defaults or dividend cuts. Risk management strategies, such as diversification and due diligence, are essential.

Conclusion

Income investing offers a methodical approach to building a portfolio that generates a reliable stream of income. Whether you're seeking income to cover living expenses or reinvest for future growth, income investing can provide financial stability and peace of mind. As with any investment strategy, it's important to align income investing with your financial goals, risk tolerance, and time horizon. In the following chapters, we will explore additional investment strategies and tactics to help you refine your investment approach.

Chapter 12: Risk and Reward: Finding the Right Balance

Investing inherently involves a trade-off between risk and reward. Striking the right balance is crucial for building a successful investment portfolio. In this chapter, we will explore the dynamics of risk and reward in investing, strategies for managing risk, and how to align your investment choices with your financial goals.

Understanding Risk and Reward

The Risk-Return Trade-Off

The relationship between risk and reward is a fundamental concept in investing. Generally, assets with higher potential returns also come with higher levels of risk. Investors must decide how much risk they are willing to take on to achieve their desired returns.

Types of Risk

Investors face various types of risk, including:

- **Market Risk:** The risk of losing money due to broad market movements.
- **Company Risk:** The risk associated with individual companies or stocks.
- **Interest Rate Risk:** The risk that changes in interest rates will affect the value of bonds and other fixed-income securities.
- **Inflation Risk:** The risk that rising prices will erode the purchasing power of your investments.
- **Liquidity Risk:** The risk of not being able to sell an investment quickly at a fair price.

Balancing Risk and Reward

Risk Tolerance

Your risk tolerance is a critical factor in determining the level of risk you can comfortably take on. It is influenced by factors such as your financial goals, time horizon, and personal preferences. Understanding your risk tolerance is essential for aligning your investments with your comfort level.

Asset Allocation

Asset allocation is a key strategy for balancing risk and reward. By diversifying your portfolio across different asset classes, such as stocks, bonds, and cash equivalents, you can manage risk while pursuing your financial goals.

Risk Management Strategies

Risk management techniques, such as setting stop-loss orders, using hedging strategies, and maintaining an emergency fund, can help mitigate potential losses and provide a safety net during market downturns.

Aligning Investments with Goals

Short-Term vs. Long-Term Goals

Consider the time horizon of your financial goals when making investment decisions. Long-term goals may allow for a higher allocation to growth-oriented assets, while short-term goals may require a more conservative approach.

Risk-Adjusted Returns

Evaluate investments based on their risk-adjusted returns, which consider the level of risk taken to achieve a certain level of return. Some investments may offer better risk-adjusted returns than others.

Diversification

Reducing Single-Asset Risk

Diversifying your portfolio across different asset classes, industries, and geographic regions can help reduce the risk associated with holding a single investment.

Benefits of Diversification

Diversification can provide stability during market volatility and protect your portfolio from the poor performance of any one asset. It can also enhance your chances of achieving your financial goals.

Conclusion

Balancing risk and reward is a fundamental aspect of investing. By understanding your risk tolerance, implementing asset allocation strategies, and managing risk effectively, you can build a portfolio that aligns with your financial goals while mitigating potential downsides. Remember that risk is an inherent part of investing, but thoughtful risk management can help you navigate the complexities of the financial markets with confidence. In the following chapters, we will delve deeper into specific investment strategies and tactics to help you make informed and balanced investment decisions.

Chapter 13: Market Research and Analysis

In the dynamic world of stock market investing, staying informed and conducting thorough research is essential. This chapter explores the importance of market research and analysis, the various tools and techniques available, and how to use them to make informed investment decisions.

The Role of Market Research

Informed Decision-Making

Market research provides the information and insights you need to make informed investment decisions. It helps you understand market trends, identify opportunities, and assess risks.

Continuous Learning

The stock market is constantly evolving. Engaging in ongoing research and analysis is a way to stay ahead of the curve and adapt to changing market conditions.

Types of Market Research

Fundamental Analysis

Fundamental analysis involves evaluating a company's financial health and prospects to determine its intrinsic value. Key elements include analyzing financial statements, earnings reports, and economic indicators.

Technical Analysis

Technical analysis relies on historical price and volume data to predict future price movements. It involves studying charts, patterns, and technical indicators to make trading decisions.

Macroeconomic Analysis

Macroeconomic analysis assesses the broader economic environment, including factors such as interest rates, inflation, and geopolitical events. These factors can impact the overall market and specific industries.

Industry Research

Understanding specific industries and sectors is crucial for identifying investment opportunities. Industry research helps you assess the competitive landscape, growth potential, and risks within a particular sector.

Tools and Techniques

Financial News and Media

Staying updated with financial news outlets, websites, and television programs is a straightforward way to access market information and expert analysis.

Company Reports

Company reports, including annual reports and quarterly filings, provide detailed financial information and insights into a company's operations and performance.

Stock Screeners

Stock screeners allow you to filter and search for stocks based on specific criteria, such as P/E ratios, dividend yields, or market capitalization.

Technical Analysis Software

Technical analysis software provides tools for charting, technical indicator analysis, and pattern recognition to aid in making trading decisions.

Economic Calendars

Economic calendars track important economic events, such as central bank announcements and economic data releases, which can impact financial markets.

Conducting Market Analysis

Research Goals

Clearly define your research goals. Are you seeking long-term investments, short-term trades, or income-generating assets? Your goals will shape your research approach.

Information Gathering

Gather information from multiple sources to get a well-rounded view of the market. Avoid relying solely on one source of information.

Risk Assessment

Assess the risks associated with potential investments. Consider factors such as market volatility, industry-specific risks, and company-specific risks.

Long-Term vs. Short-Term Analysis

Tailor your analysis to your investment horizon. Long-term investors may focus on fundamental analysis, while short-term traders may emphasize technical analysis.

Conclusion

Market research and analysis are integral parts of successful stock market investing. By consistently conducting research, staying informed, and using various tools and techniques, you can make well-informed investment decisions that align with your financial goals and risk tolerance. Keep in mind that the investment landscape is ever-evolving, and continuous learning and adaptation are key to achieving investment success. In the following chapters, we will explore specific investment strategies and tactics to help you put your research and analysis into practice.

Chapter 14: Investment Strategies for Retirement Planning

Retirement planning is a long-term financial goal that requires careful consideration and strategic investment decisions. This chapter explores various investment strategies specifically tailored to help you achieve a financially secure and comfortable retirement.

The Importance of Retirement Planning

Changing Retirement Landscape

With increasing life expectancies and changes in pension systems, individuals are increasingly responsible for funding their own retirements. Effective retirement planning is essential to ensure you have the financial resources needed to enjoy your retirement years.

Compound Interest Advantage

Starting early and consistently contributing to your retirement accounts can harness the power of compound interest, which allows your investments to grow exponentially over time.

Retirement Investment Strategies

Determine Retirement Goals

Before selecting specific investment strategies, clarify your retirement goals. Consider factors such as when you want to retire, your desired retirement lifestyle, and any anticipated expenses.

Asset Allocation

Asset allocation is a critical component of retirement planning. It involves distributing your investments among different asset classes, such as stocks, bonds, and cash equivalents, to balance risk and return.

Time Horizon

Your retirement timeline plays a significant role in asset allocation. The longer your time horizon, the more risk you can afford to take on by allocating a higher percentage of your portfolio to stocks for potential long-term growth.

Diversification

Diversification within asset classes and across sectors can help reduce risk. It prevents your retirement portfolio from being overly dependent on the performance of a single investment.

Income-Generating Assets

Consider including income-generating assets, such as dividend-paying stocks or bonds, in your retirement portfolio to provide a consistent cash flow during retirement.

Tax-Efficient Strategies

Be mindful of the tax implications of your retirement investments. Utilize tax-advantaged accounts like IRAs and 401(k)s to minimize your tax burden and maximize your retirement savings.

Retirement Investment Vehicles

Employer-Sponsored Plans

Take advantage of employer-sponsored retirement plans, such as 401(k)s, if available. These plans often include employer contributions and provide tax benefits.

Individual Retirement Accounts (IRAs)

IRAs offer tax advantages and flexibility. Traditional IRAs provide tax-deferred growth, while Roth IRAs offer tax-free withdrawals in retirement.

Annuities

Annuities are insurance products that can provide a guaranteed income stream in retirement. Immediate annuities start payments right away, while deferred annuities allow you to defer payments until a future date.

Retirement Withdrawal Strategies

Systematic Withdrawals

Implement a systematic withdrawal strategy in retirement to ensure you have a steady income stream. This may involve setting up regular withdrawals from retirement accounts.

Required Minimum Distributions (RMDs)

Be aware of RMD rules for tax-advantaged retirement accounts. Starting at a certain age, you are required to withdraw a minimum amount each year.

Sequence of Returns

Pay attention to the sequence of investment returns in retirement. Poor market performance early in retirement can significantly impact the longevity of your savings.

Regular Review and Adjustments

Periodic Check-Ins

Regularly review your retirement portfolio and make adjustments as needed. Changes in your financial situation or goals may require modifications to your investment strategy.

Conclusion

Effective retirement planning and investment strategies are crucial to ensuring a comfortable and financially secure retirement. By setting clear retirement goals, implementing a diversified investment approach, and taking advantage of tax-efficient retirement accounts, you can work towards achieving your retirement dreams. Remember that retirement planning is a dynamic process that requires ongoing monitoring and adjustments as your circumstances change. In the following chapters, we will explore additional investment strategies and tactics to help you fine-tune your retirement plan.

Chapter 15: Investment Strategies for Wealth Preservation

Wealth preservation is a crucial aspect of long-term financial planning. In this chapter, we will explore investment strategies specifically designed to protect and preserve your wealth, ensuring that it endures for future generations or sustains your financial security throughout your life.

The Significance of Wealth Preservation

Preserving Your Financial Legacy

Wealth preservation is about safeguarding the wealth you've accumulated over time. Whether you've built your wealth through investments, inheritances, or other means, it's essential to protect it for your benefit and that of your heirs.

Inflation and Erosion

Inflation erodes the purchasing power of money over time. Without appropriate wealth preservation strategies, your wealth's real value may decrease over the years.

Wealth Preservation Investment Strategies

Capital Preservation

Capital preservation is a primary objective of wealth preservation strategies. It focuses on protecting your initial investment to ensure that it retains its value.

Income-Generating Assets

Invest in income-generating assets such as dividend-paying stocks, bonds, and rental properties. These assets can provide a steady stream of income to cover expenses while preserving capital.

Diversification

Diversify your portfolio across different asset classes and geographic regions to spread risk. A well-diversified portfolio is less vulnerable to the poor performance of a single investment.

Conservative Investments

Consider allocating a portion of your portfolio to conservative investments, such as high-quality bonds or certificates of deposit (CDs). These provide stability and safety.

Risk Management

Implement risk management strategies, including setting stop-loss orders and employing hedging techniques to protect your investments from significant losses.

Estate Planning

Estate planning is a vital aspect of wealth preservation. Ensure your assets are distributed according to your wishes through wills, trusts, and beneficiary designations.

Tax-Efficient Strategies

Tax Planning

Be mindful of tax implications when managing your wealth. Utilize tax-efficient investment vehicles and strategies to minimize your tax burden.

Tax-Advantaged Accounts

Maximize contributions to tax-advantaged accounts, such as IRAs and 401(k)s, to benefit from tax-deferred or tax-free growth.

Long-Term Focus

Patience and Discipline

Wealth preservation often involves a long-term perspective. Be patient and disciplined in your investment decisions, avoiding impulsive reactions to short-term market fluctuations.

Ongoing Review

Regularly review your wealth preservation strategy and make necessary adjustments based on changes in your financial situation or goals.

Asset Protection

Legal Structures

Consider using legal structures such as trusts or limited liability companies (LLCs) to protect your assets from creditors or legal claims.

Conclusion

Wealth preservation is a critical component of long-term financial planning. By implementing strategies that prioritize capital preservation, generate income, and manage risk, you can protect and grow your wealth over time. Remember that wealth preservation is an ongoing process that may require adjustments as your financial circumstances evolve. Whether you aim to sustain your lifestyle in retirement, provide for future generations, or support charitable endeavors, effective wealth preservation strategies are key to achieving your financial objectives. In the following chapters, we will explore additional investment strategies and tactics to help you further refine your wealth preservation plan.